CHLOE KIM

Wo... ...ts

T0011873

MARY HERTZ SCARBROUGH

Rourke
Educational Media

A Division of
Carson
Dellosa
Education

Before Reading: *Building Background Knowledge and Vocabulary*

Building background knowledge can help children process new information and build upon what they already know. Before reading a book, it is important to tap into what children already know about the topic. This will help them develop their vocabulary and increase their reading comprehension.

Questions and Activities to Build Background Knowledge:

1. Look at the front cover of the book and read the title. What do you think this book will be about?
2. What do you already know about this topic?
3. Take a book walk and skim the pages. Look at the table of contents, photographs, captions, and bold words. Did these text features give you any information or predictions about what you will read in this book?

Vocabulary: *Vocabulary Is Key to Reading Comprehension*

Use the following directions to prompt a conversation about each word.

- Read the vocabulary words.
- What comes to mind when you see each word?
- What do you think each word means?

Vocabulary Words:
- advocates
- halfpipe
- medalist
- prevailed
- qualified
- rotations

During Reading: *Reading for Meaning and Understanding*

To achieve deep comprehension of a book, children are encouraged to use close reading strategies. During reading, it is important to have children stop and make connections. These connections result in deeper analysis and understanding of a book.

Close Reading a Text

During reading, have children stop and talk about the following:

- Any confusing parts
- Any unknown words
- Text to text, text to self, text to world connections
- The main idea in each chapter or heading

Encourage children to use context clues to determine the meaning of any unknown words. These strategies will help children learn to analyze the text more thoroughly as they read.

When you are finished reading this book, turn to the next-to-last page for After Reading Questions and an Activity.

TABLE OF CONTENTS

TAKING FLIGHT

She's a champion snowboarder who doesn't really like snow! That's Chloe Kim. After all, she does come from sunny Southern California—the land of beaches.

Chloe started snowboarding with her father when she was just four years old. Early in the morning on Saturdays, he'd buckle her into the back seat and drive five or six hours to Mammoth Mountain.

Three Languages

Chloe's parents sent her to Switzerland so that she could learn to speak French. In addition to English and French, she speaks Korean. Her parents are from South Korea, and she still has relatives who live there.

Chloe was soon better than her dad, and she began competing at age six. She practiced hard. She even practiced jumping on a trampoline while on her snowboard!

Chloe was in the third grade when she moved to Switzerland to live with her aunt, but she never stopped snowboarding. She woke up at four o'clock in the morning, took two trains to reach a **halfpipe** in the French Alps, and continued her training.

halfpipe (haf-pipe): a U-shaped trench of snow

FLYING HIGH

By 2014, Chloe was competing around the world. The eighth-grader frequently earned top scores. She dreamed of competing in the Olympics. However, under Olympic rules, she was too young to compete at the Games in Sochi, Russia, that year.

Instead, Chloe kept practicing. She kept competing. And she kept winning medals.

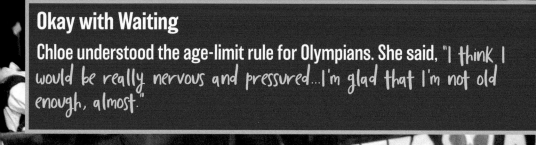

Okay with Waiting

Chloe understood the age-limit rule for Olympians. She said, "I think I would be really nervous and pressured...I'm glad that I'm not old enough, almost."

At the 2014 X Games, Chloe won a silver medal in the halfpipe event and became the youngest X Games **medalist** at the time. She finished second to Kelly Clark, who went on to win a bronze medal in the Sochi games.

Left to right: Chloe, Kelly, and Kaitlyn Farrington

At the 2015 X Games, Chloe beat Kelly and became the competition's youngest gold medalist.

medalist (MED-uh-list): an athlete or other person who is awarded a medal

In 2016, Chloe made history on the halfpipe. In a competition in the state of Utah, she won after doing back-to-back 1080s. That means she completed three full **rotations** nearly 35 feet (10.7 meters) off the ground. Then, she immediately did the move again! These back-to-back 1080s—and her perfect score of 100— were firsts in women's snowboarding.

rotations (ROH-tay-shuhnz): complete turns or spins

Chloe also won gold at the 2016 X Games in Oslo, Norway.

Left to right: Emily Arthur, Chloe, and Yu-Rim Jeong

After her record-setting performance in Utah, Chloe participated in the 2016 Youth Olympic Games in Lillehammer, Norway. The Youth Olympic Games are for athletes from ages 15 to 18. She won gold medals in the halfpipe and slopestyle events. She also carried the flag for the United States in the opening ceremony, the first Team USA snowboarder to have that honor.

Chloe easily **qualified** for the 2018 Winter Olympics. Everyone expected her to do well in the halfpipe event. She did not disappoint.

Her first run during the finals gave her a comfortable lead. She fell on her second run. On her third run, she scored a whopping 98.25 out of 100 and completed back-to-back 1080s.

She Is Her Biggest Competitor

Chloe would have won a gold medal even without completing that third run. She said: "I didn't want to leave with the gold knowing that I could have done better. I wanted to try and do back-to-back 1080s."

qualified (KWAHL-uh-fide): having met specific requirements or conditions; eligible

The Pyeongchang, South Korea, location of the 2018 Olympics was particularly meaningful for Chloe, who is Korean-American. Her grandmother and other family members who still live in South Korea were there for her event. Chloe said she felt as though she were representing both countries.

Social Media Star

Between Instagram, Twitter, and YouTube, Chloe has more than a million followers. During the 2018 Olympics, she tweeted between runs that she was "hangry." She got thousands of retweets and likes.

Chloe's success continued. By the time she won gold in the halfpipe event at the 2019 World Championships, her winning streak had stretched for more than a year. In addition to her first World Championship title, she also **prevailed** at the 2018 and 2019 X Games.

prevailed (pri-VAYLD): overcame or won despite difficulties

Chloe continued to break boundaries. While training in Switzerland in October 2018, Chloe landed a trick called a frontside double cork 1080. She is the first woman to perform it in training successfully. She almost landed it at the 2019 World Championships, and it's only a matter of time until she succeeds.

SOARING INTO THE FUTURE

Chloe uses her fame to talk about issues that matter to her. Bullying is one topic she feels strongly about because she experienced it when she was young.

She is also associated with Protect Our Winters. The organization aims to inspire people to be **advocates** for climate change awareness.

advocates (AD-vuh-kits): supporters and promoters for a cause

Chloe decided to take a break during the 2019–2020 competition season. She wanted to adjust to college life at Princeton University. After years of homeschooling, she couldn't wait to have classmates once again. Chloe loves science classes, especially chemistry.

She plans to train for the 2022 Olympics in Beijing, China. However, she doesn't think she'll compete beyond that.

The 2022 Olympics might be Chloe's last, but she wants to keep moving at top speed. She explained: "I have so much I want to do in my life. I want to be a lawyer, I want to be a scientist, a doctor, all of these crazy things I want to try."

Chloe throws the starting pitch at a Dodgers game.

Memory Game

Look at the pictures. What do you remember reading on the pages where each image appeared?

Index

After Reading Questions

1. What do you think it takes to be one of the greatest athletes in the world? Did your ideas change after reading this book? Explain.

2. Did you learn anything about Chloe that surprised you?

3. In what ways do you think you are similar to Chloe?

4. What are two issues outside of snowboarding that Chloe cares about?

5. Why did Chloe feel she was representing both South Korea and the U.S. at the 2018 Olympics?

Activity

Imagine you're an Olympic athlete. Which events are you competing in? Why did you choose those events? Do you feel as if you are representing one country, or more than one? Write a journal entry to explain your answers.

About the Author

Mary Hertz Scarbrough is inspired by Chloe Kim's talent, hard work, and success. She has a husband, three young adult daughters, and two rescue dogs, and she is looking forward to breaking out her cross-country skis in the near future. She's also enjoyed downhill skiing on occasion but doesn't anticipate ever being able to stand up, let alone go anywhere, on a snowboard.

www.rourkeeducationalmedia.com

Quote sources: Branch, John, "Among the Best, but Having to Wait," the New York Times. January 19, 2014: https://www.nytimes.com/2014/01/19/sports/amid-giggles-a-snowboarding-wizard.html ; Reid, Scott, "Chloe Kim wins gold for U.S. in Olympic halfpipe," Pasadena Star-News: February 12, 2018: https://www.pasadenastarnews.com/2018/02/12/chloe-kim-wins-gold-for-u-s-in-olympic-halfpipe/ ; Pinelli, Brian, "Chole Kim's Next Big Challenge: College," the New York Times, February 12, 2019: https://www.nytimes.com/2019/02/12/sports/chloe-kim-halfpipe-world-championships.html

PHOTO CREDITS: page 5: ©aflosports, Hiroyuki Sato; page 6-7: ©So-CoAddict; page 9: ©aflosports, Hiroyuki Sato; page 10-11: ©ZUMA Wire, ©aflosports, Hiroyuki Sato; page 12-13: ©rhyman007; page 14-15: ©NTB Scanpix, All Rights Reserved; page 16-17: Newscom; page 18-19: ©1980-2018 YONHAPNEWS AGENCY. All rights reserved; page 20-21: Newscom; page 22-23: Newscom; page 24-25: ©Jag_cz; page 26-27: Newscom; page 28-29: ©Icon Sportswire (A Division of XML Team Solutions) All Rights Reserved, ©Admedia

Edited by: Madison Capitano
Cover and interior design by: Rhea Magaro-Wallace

Library of Congress PCN Data

Chloe Kim / Mary Hertz Scarbrough
(Women in Sports)
ISBN 978-1-73163-829-8 (hard cover)
ISBN 978-1-73163-906-6 (soft cover)
ISBN 978-1-73163-983-7 (e-Book)
ISBN 978-1-73164-060-4 (ePub)
Library of Congress Control Number: 2020930211

Rourke Educational Media
Printed in the United States of America
03-1062411937